I LOVE YOU MORE THAN TRASH

RP STUDIO
PHILADELPHIA

Let yourself be loved, you

_____

_____.

When you bare your teeth at me, I think of

_____.

The

_____

**on your chin glistens,
and I can't help but**

_____.

I'll always treasure your

_____

like that time we

_____

in the

_____.

As we scamper to the

_____,
the glint in your eye fills me with

_____.

You are the

_____

_____

human I've ever known.

I enjoy playing dead
with you, but I love

_____

even more.

As the city falls asleep,
our friendship radiates

_____.

We travel to the most exotic places, like

_____ and

_____.

You really

_____ me.

The satisfaction we get from sharing

_____

puts me in a primal trance.

I like how you care so

_____

about

_____.

It gives me hope for the future.

_____:

**Self-actualization or self-indulgence?
Either way, I'm**

_____.

You pressure me to

_____,

and honestly, it's

_____.

We both glare at

_____,

and that makes me feel

_____.

You have infected me with your

_____.

Our nighttime escapades leave me

_____.

Catching

_____

**with you is the foundation
of our friendship.**

Where I see

_____,

you see

_____,

and that moves me to tears.

The roaring static of your

_____

drowns out my

_____.

In this

_____

you are my

_____.

**When you let me have
that butter-soaked**

_____,

**I knew we would
be friends forever.**

Soggy pizza crust helps me appreciate

_____.

Life will shoo us away, but our

_____ will

_____ us.

The way you risked your tail for that

_____

brings me great joy.

I'm proud of your

_____.

The tranquil act of gathering

_____

brings us together.

You are so

_____!

The way you snatched that

_____

out of that

_____

was terrific!

I always feel

_____

when I see your filthy

_____.

I follow your

_____

like morsels of

_____

left behind.

I appreciate your harsh vibes toward

_____.

When you give me that

_____

look, I

_____.

That coquettish smile when you find

_____

in a

_____

is everything.

Hot Fresh Pizza

You are a magnet for

_____,
**and it makes me feel
vulnerable yet safe.**

You smell like

_____,

and it's glorious!

Let's suspend what little

_____

we have left and

_____

all weekend.

Your

_____

is the bountiful

_____

in my life.

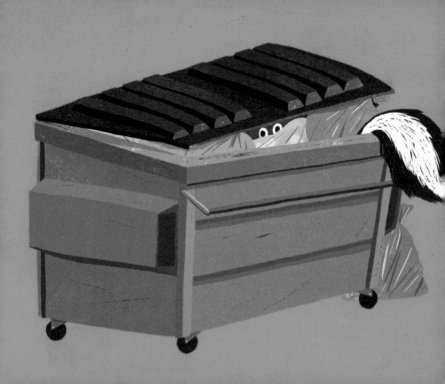

Sloshing around in

_____

is one of my perfect memories of us.

Your inexplicable urge to

_____

keeps me sane.

Our shared

_____

of

_____

warms my belly.

You have a nose for

_____,

and it beats my

_____

any night.

Naps are

_____,

knowing you are

_____.

You bring me

_____

during those disquieting hours before

_____ .

You indulge my conspiracies about

_____,

and that makes me feel seen.

Savor that

_____.

You deserve

_____

and so much more.

We agreed to pretend that

_____

didn't happen, and that's okay.

There is nothing wrong with a little

_____.

Let's live it up!

TRASH PANDA, YOU'RE MY TREASURE!

RP Studio™
Hachette Book Group
1290 Avenue of the Americas, New York, NY 10104
www.runningpress.com
@Running_Press

Printed in China

First Edition: October 2023

Published by RP Studio, an imprint of Perseus Books, LLC, a subsidiary of Hachette Book Group, Inc. The RP Studio name and logo are trademarks of the Hachette Book Group.

Running Press books may be purchased in bulk for business, educational, or promotional use. For more information, please contact your local bookseller or the Hachette Book Group Special Markets Department at Special.Markets@hbgusa.com.

The publisher is not responsible for websites (or their content) that are not owned by the publisher.

Text by Alexander Schneider
Design by Justine Kelley

ISBN: 978-0-7624-8434-8

APS

10 9 8 7 6 5 4 3 2 1